POP PIANO HITS

SIMPLE ARRANGEMENTS FOR STUDENTS OF ALL AGES

Memories, Truth Hurts & More Hot Singles

ISBN 978-1-5400-8244-2

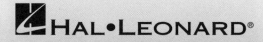

Visit Hal Leonard Online at
www.halleonard.com

Contact us:
Hal Leonard
7777 West Bluemound Road
Milwaukee, WI 53213
Email: info@halleonard.com

In Europe, contact:
Hal Leonard Europe Limited
42 Wigmore Street
Marylebone, London, W1U 2RN
Email: info@halleonardeurope.com

In Australia, contact:
Hal Leonard Australia Pty. Ltd.
4 Lentara Court
Cheltenham, Victoria, 3192 Australia
Email: info@halleonard.com.au

Contents

BEAUTIFUL PEOPLE

Words and Music by ED SHEERAN,
KHALID ROBINSON, FRED GIBSON,
MAX MARTIN and SHELLBACK

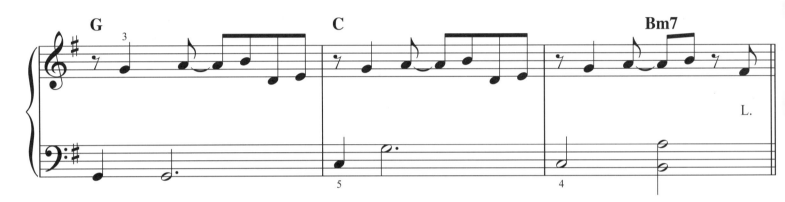

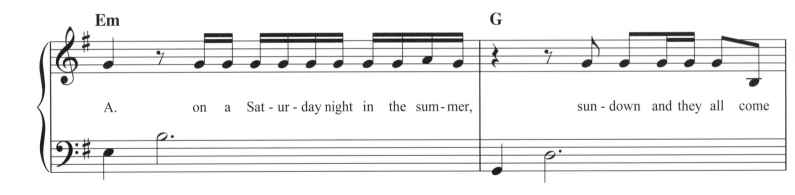

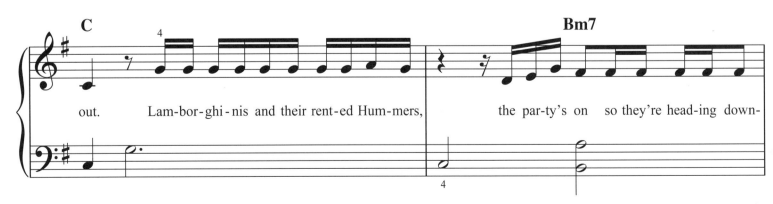

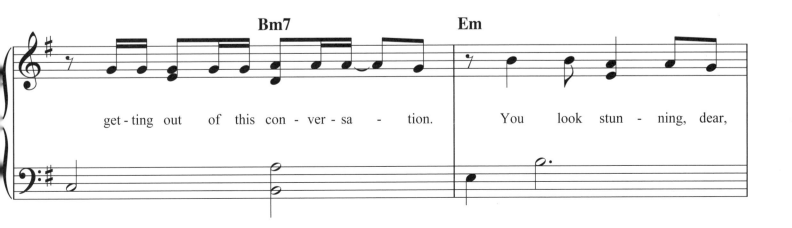

so don't ask that ques - tion here. This is my on - ly fear,

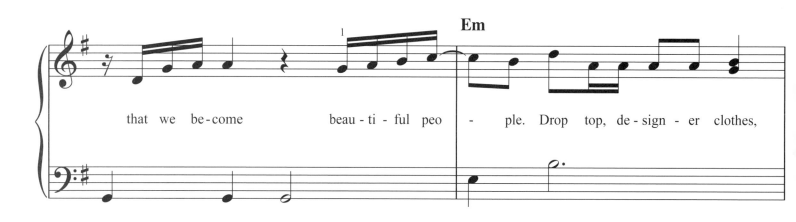

that we be-come beau - ti - ful peo - ple. Drop top, de - sign - er clothes,

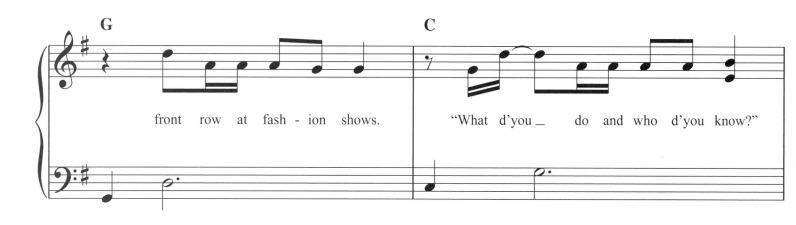

front row at fash - ion shows. "What d'you __ do and who d'you know?"

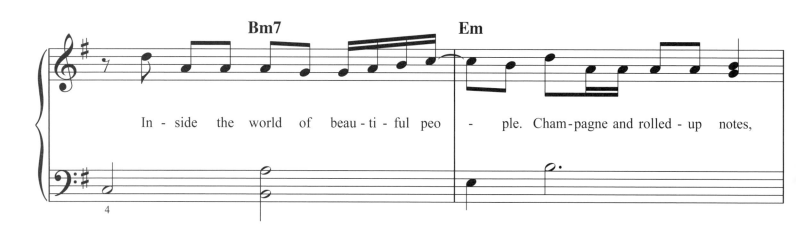

In - side the world of beau - ti - ful peo - ple. Cham-pagne and rolled - up notes,

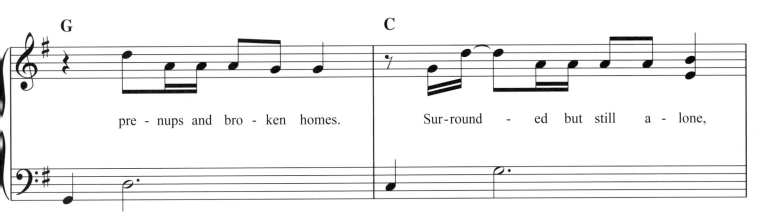

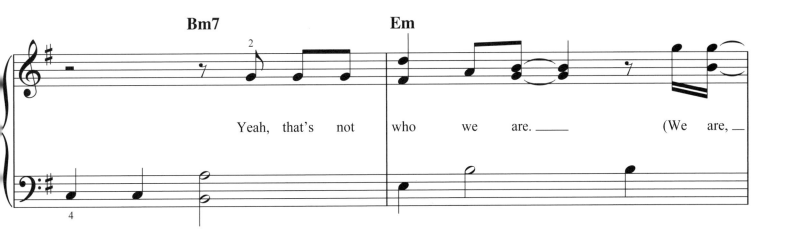

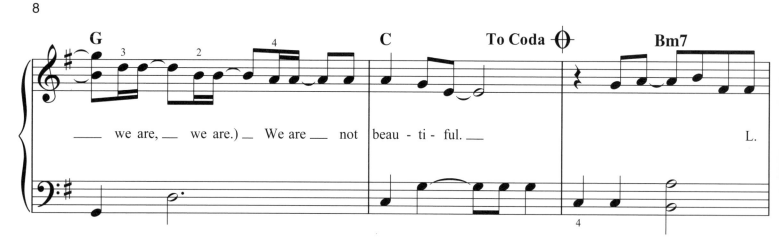

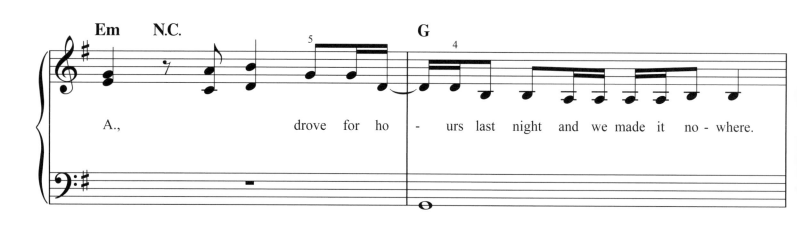

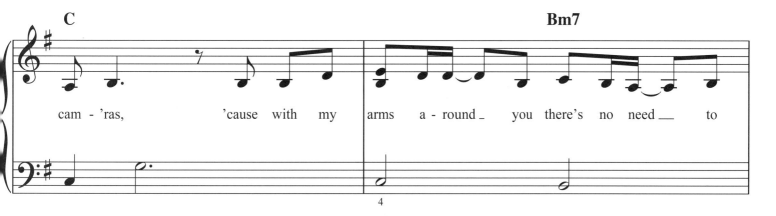

cam - 'ras,   'cause with my   arms a - round_ you there's no need _ to

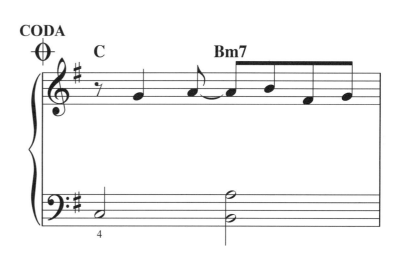

care. We don't fit in well

(We are, _ we are, _ we are.)   We are _ not

beau - ti - ful. _

LOSE YOU TO LOVE ME

Words and Music by SELENA GOMEZ,
JUSTIN TRANTER, JULIA MICHAELS,
ROBIN FREDRIKSSON and MATTIAS LARSSON

Slowly, in 2

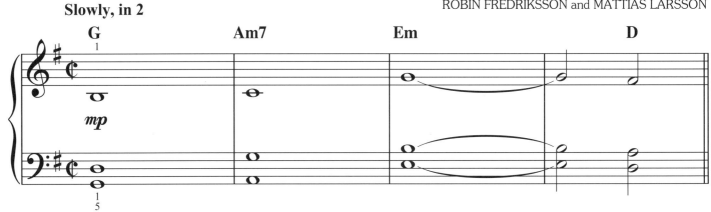

You prom-ised the world and I fell for it.
I saw the signs and I ig - nored it.

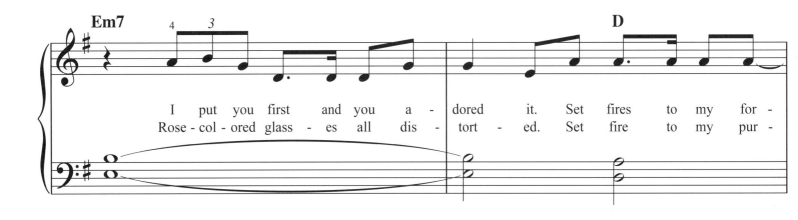

I put you first and you a - dored it. Set fires to my for-
Rose-col-ored glass-es all dis - tort - ed. Set fire to my pur-

- est, and you let it burn.
- pose, and I let it burn.
Sang off-key in my cho -
You got off on the hurt -

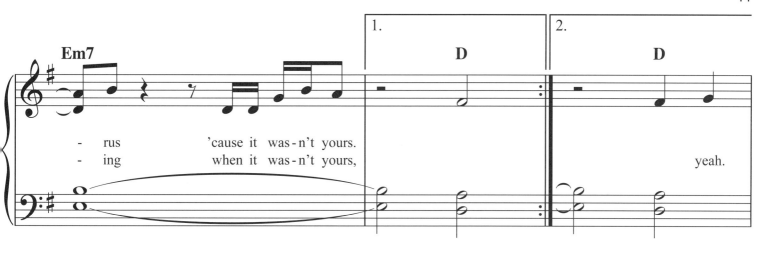

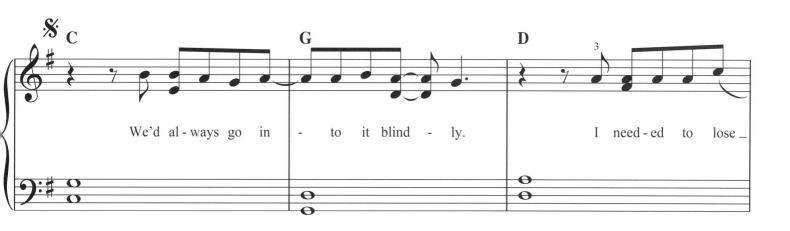

love, love, yeah, to love, yeah. I need-ed to lose ___ you to love ___ me, yeah.

To love, love, yeah, to love, love, yeah, to love, yeah. I need-ed to lose ___

To Coda

___ you to love ___ me. I gave my all and they all know it.

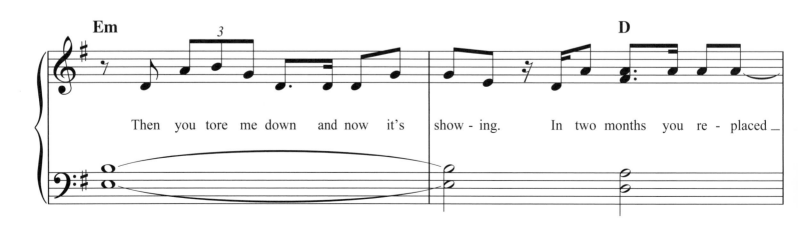

Then you tore me down and now it's show - ing. In two months you re - placed ___

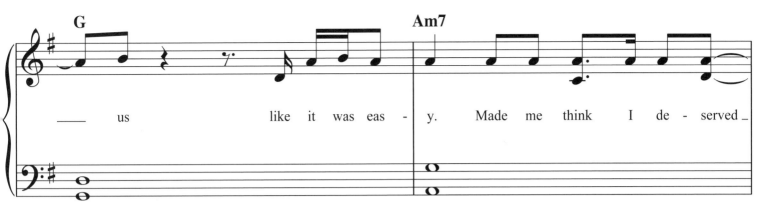

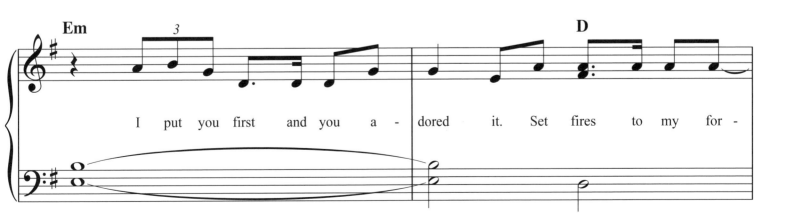

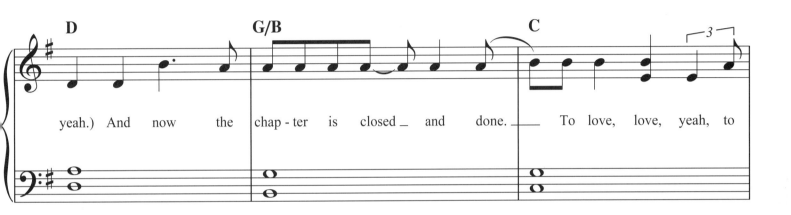

MEMORIES

Words and Music by ADEM LEVINE,
JONATHAN BELLION, JORDAN JOHNSON,
JACOB HINDLIN, STEFAN JOHNSON,
MICHAEL POLLACK and VINCENT FORD

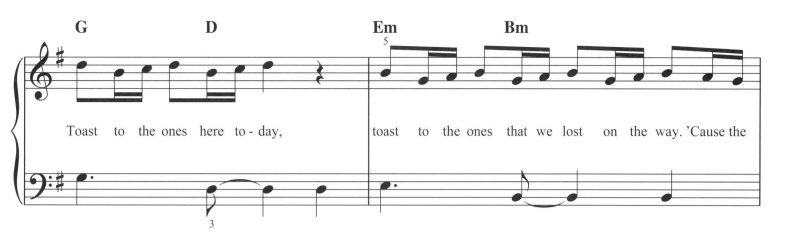

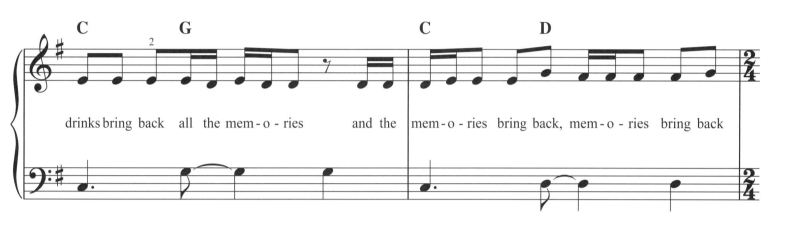

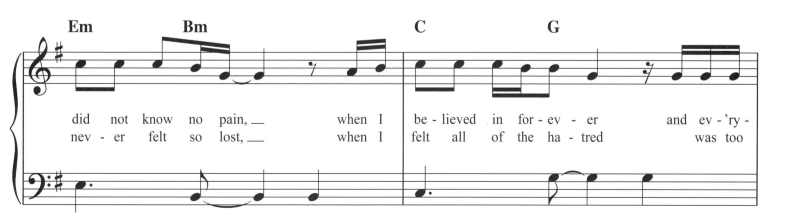

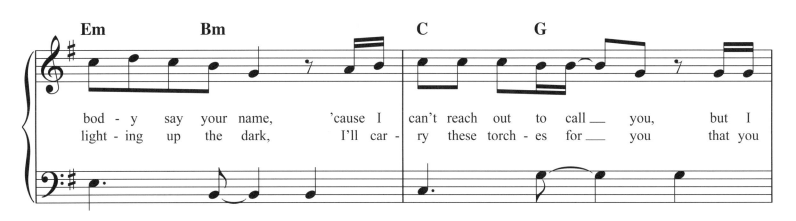

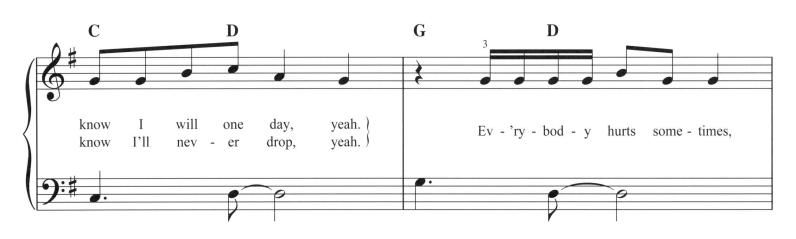

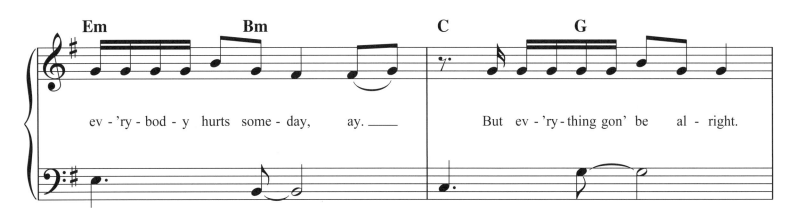

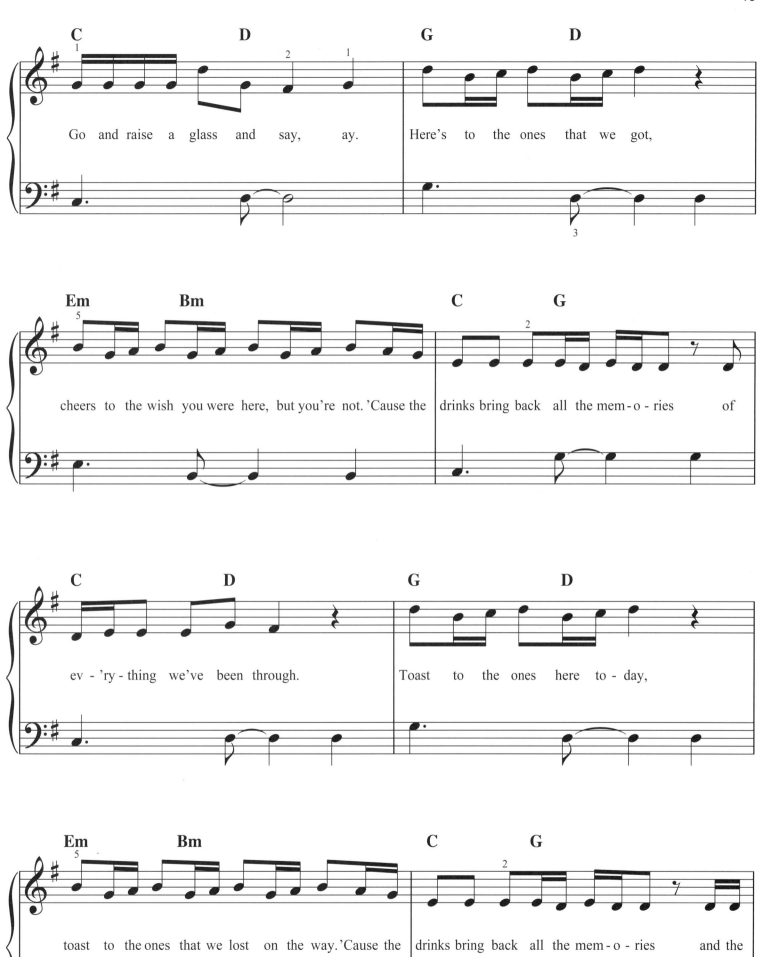

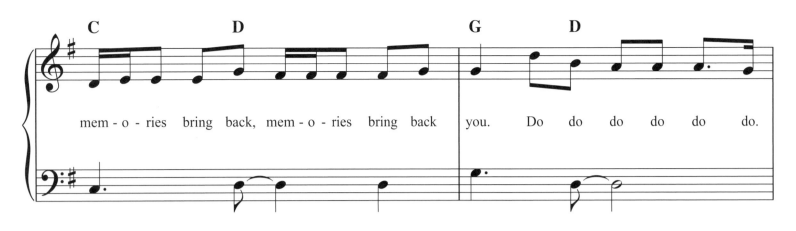

mem - o - ries bring back, mem - o - ries bring back you. Do do do do do do.

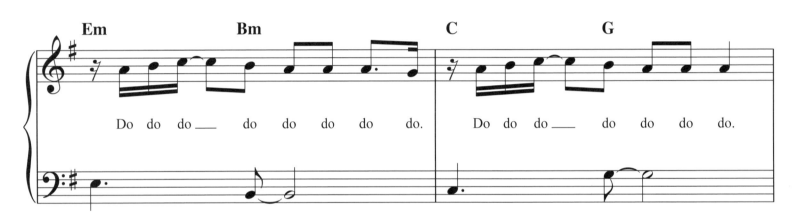

Do do do ___ do do do do do. Do do do ___ do do do do.

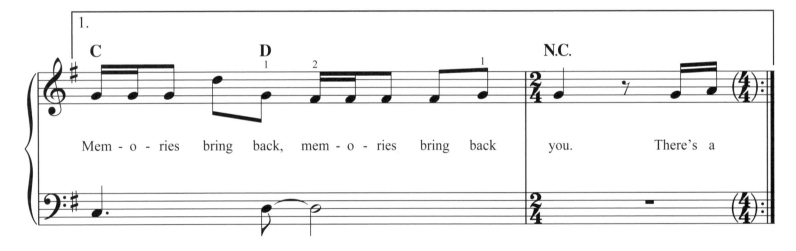

1.

Mem - o - ries bring back, mem - o - ries bring back you. There's a

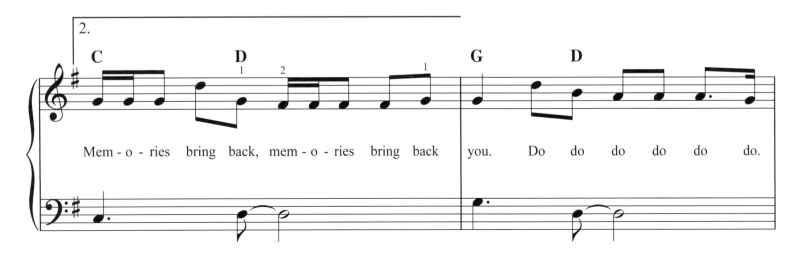

2.

Mem - o - ries bring back, mem - o - ries bring back you. Do do do do do do.

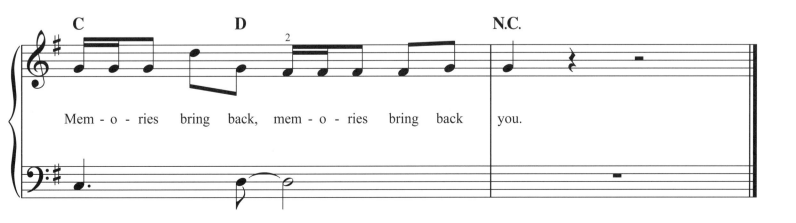

10,000 HOURS

Words and Music by DAN SMYERS,
JORDAN REYNOLDS, SHAY MOONEY,
JUSTIN BIEBER, JASON BOYD
and JESSIE JO DILLON

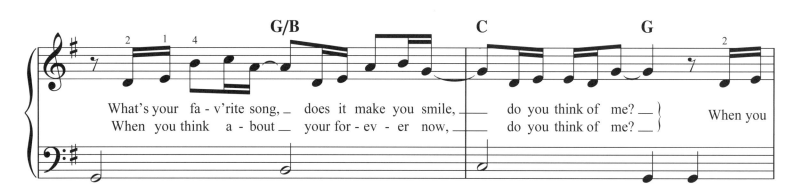

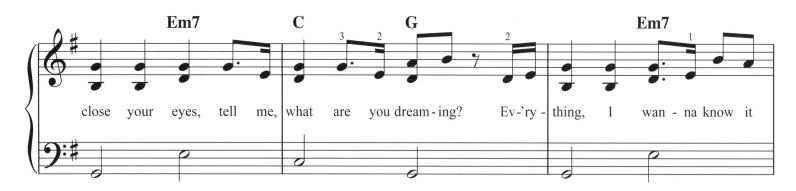

all, _____ mmm. __ I'd spend ten thou - sand ho - urs ____ and

ten thou - sand more, __ oh, if that's what it takes __ to learn that

sweet heart of yours. __ And I might nev - er get __ there, ___ but

I'm gon - na try, _____ if it's ten thou - sand ho - urs or the

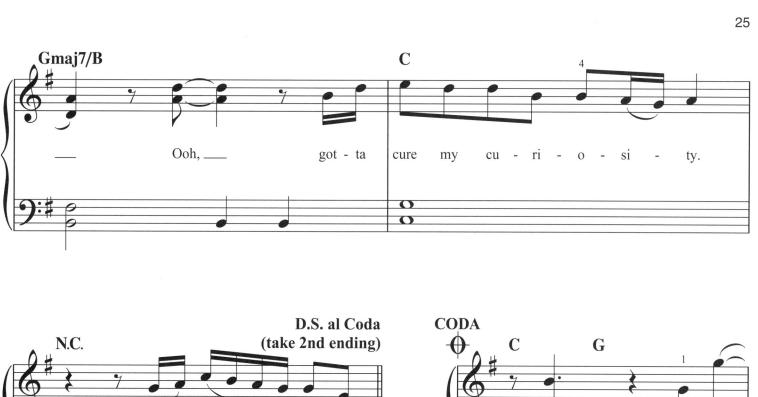

Ooh, ___ got - ta cure my cu - ri - o - si - ty.

Oh, ___ yeah. ___ I'd spend

Yeah. And I, ___

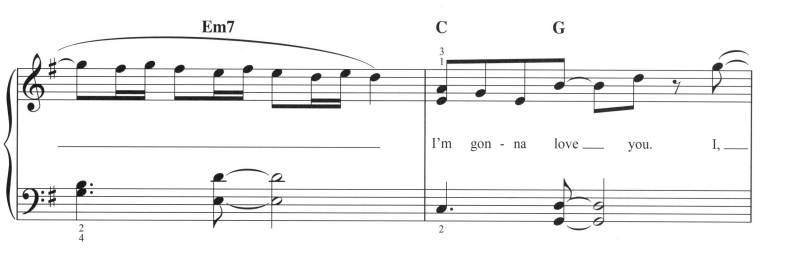

I'm gon - na love ___ you. I, ___

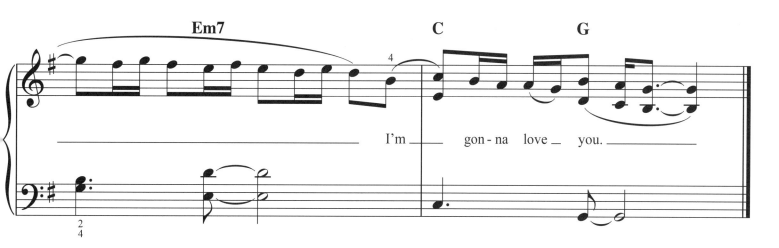

I'm ___ gon - na love ___ you. ___

TRUTH HURTS

Words and Music by LIZZO,
Eric Frederic, JESSE ST. JOHN GELLER
and STEVEN CHEUNG

Moderately, in 2

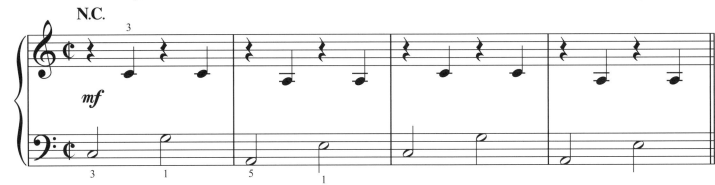

Why men great 'til they got-ta be great? *Woo!*

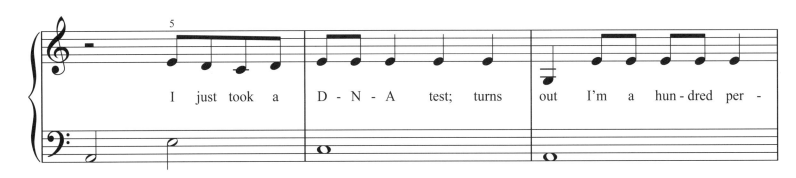

I just took a D-N-A test; turns out I'm a hun-dred per-

cent that kid e-ven when I'm cry-in' cra-zy. Yeah, I got boy prob-lems, that's the

hu - man in me. ___ Bling, bling, then I solve 'em, that's the god-dess in me. You could - a had a

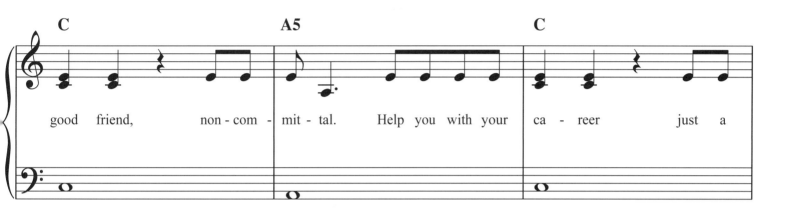

good friend, non - com - mit - tal. Help you with your ca - reer just a

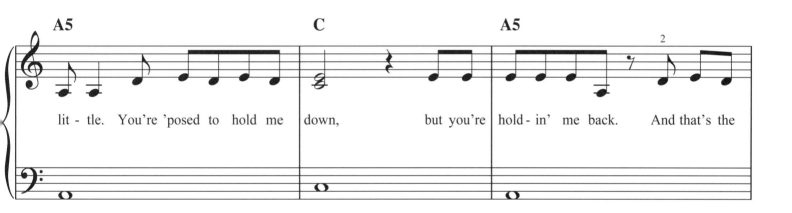

lit - tle. You're 'posed to hold me down, but you're hold - in' me back. And that's the

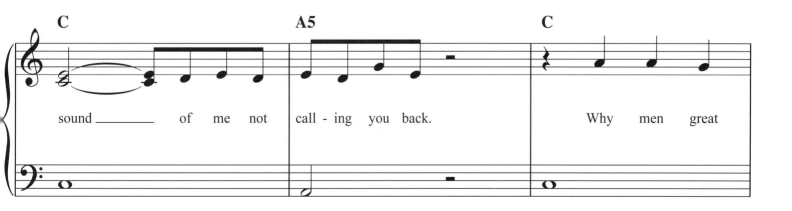

sound _____ of me not call - ing you back. Why men great

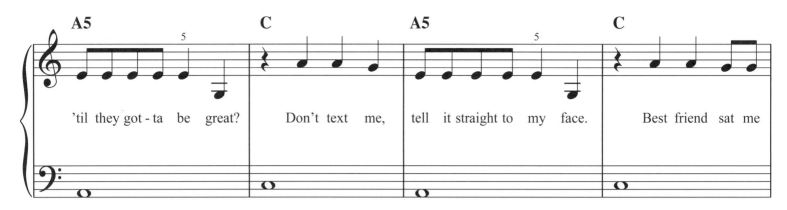

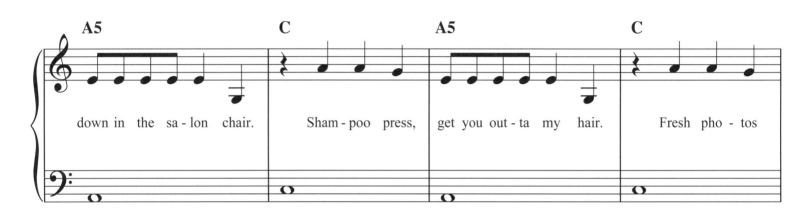

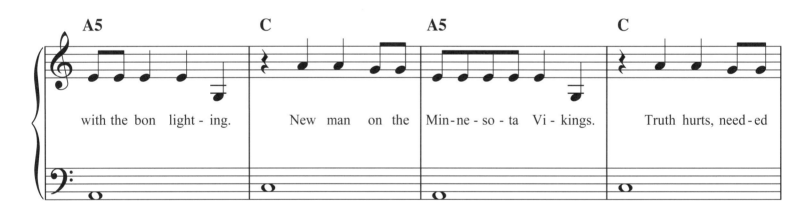

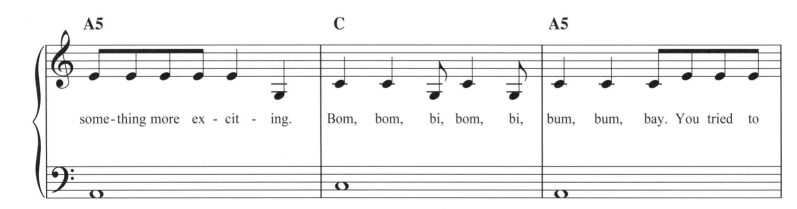

break my heart. _ Oh, that | breaks my heart _ that you | thought you ev - er had it. No, you

ain't from the start. _ Hey, I'm | glad you're back with your friends. I mean, | who would wan - na hide this? I will

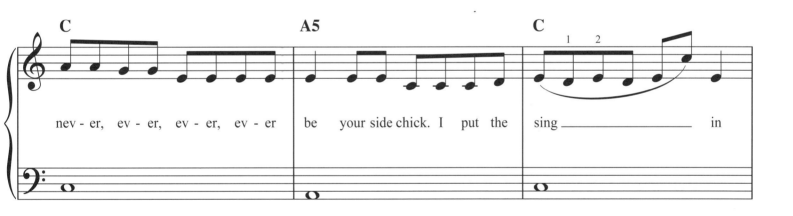

nev - er, ev - er, ev - er, ev - er | be your side chick. I put the | sing _____ in

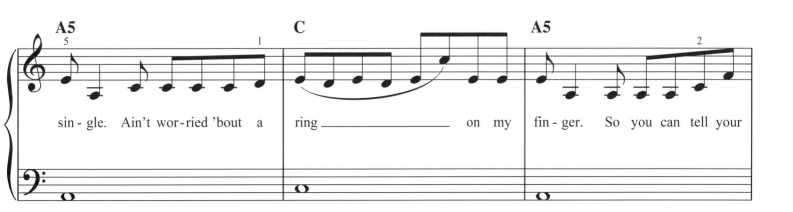

sin - gle. Ain't wor-ried 'bout a | ring _____ on my | fin - ger. So you can tell your

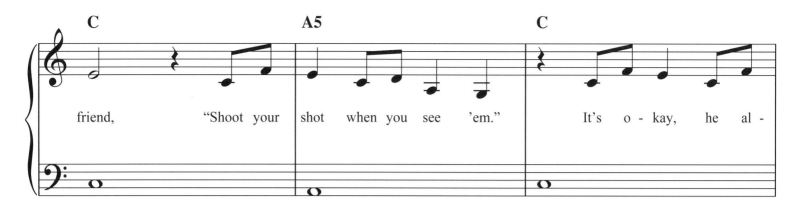

C   **A5**   **C**

friend,   "Shoot your   shot when you see 'em."   It's o - kay, he al -

A5   **C**   **A5**

read - y knows my feel - ings.   Why men great   'til they got - ta be great?

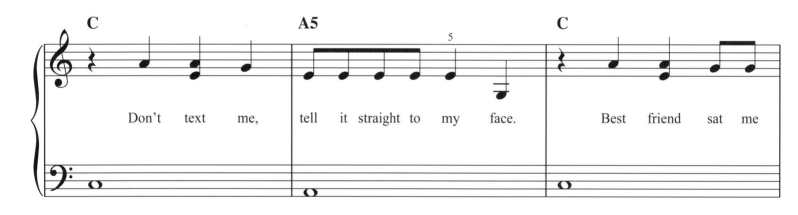

C   **A5**   **C**

Don't text me,   tell it straight to my face.   Best friend sat me

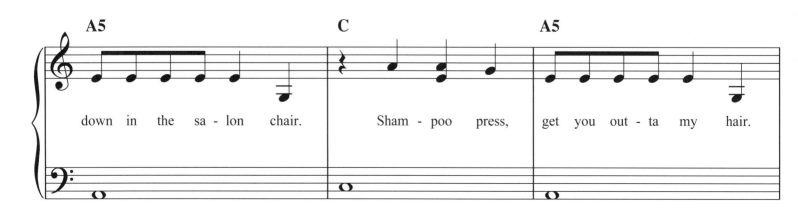

A5   **C**   **A5**

down in the sa - lon chair.   Sham - poo press,   get you out - a my hair.

Fresh pho - tos with the bon light - ing. New man on the

Min - ne - so - ta Vi - kings. Truth hurts, need - ed some-thing more ex - cit - ing.

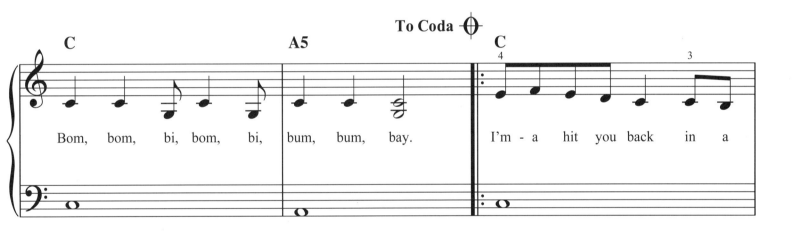

Bom, bom, bi bom, bi, bum, bum, bay. I'm - a hit you back in a

min - ute. I don't play ___ tag, yeah, I been it.

We don't deal with lies, we don't do good-byes. We just keep it push-in' like

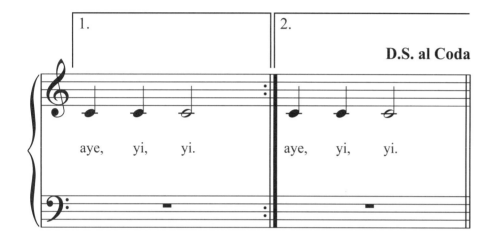

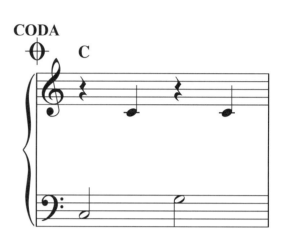

1. aye, yi, yi.

2. **D.S. al Coda** aye, yi, yi.

CODA C

With the bomb light - ing._____ Min - ne - so - ta

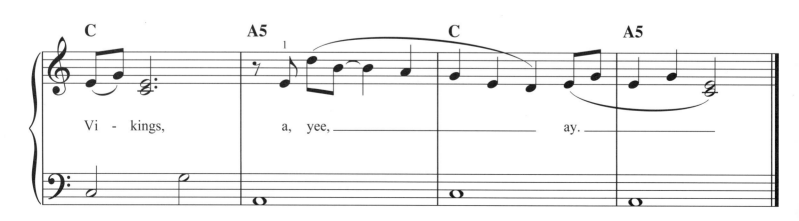

Vi - kings, a, yee,_____ ay._____